Playing with Scales

A FRESH WAY TO PRACTISE SCALES!

LEVEL ONE

CLARINET

Devised and arranged
by Alistair Watson

T0056618

CHESTER MUSIC
part of The Music Sales Group
London / New York / Paris / Sydney / Copenhagen /
Berlin / Madrid / Hong Kong / Tokyo

Published by
Chester Music
14-15 Berners Street, London W1T 3LJ, UK.

Exclusive Distributors:
Music Sales Limited
Distribution Centre, Newmarket Road,
Bury St Edmunds, Suffolk IP33 3YB, UK.
Music Sales Pty Limited
Units 3-4, 17 Willfox Street, Condell Park,
NSW 2200, Australia.

Order No. CH82082
ISBN: 978-1-78305-485-5
This book © Copyright 2014 Wise Publications,
a division of Music Sales Limited.

Edited by Jenni Norey.
Devised and arranged by Alistair Watson.
Cover design by Fresh Lemon.
Printed in the EU.

Your Guarantee of Quality:

As publishers, we strive to produce every book
to the highest commercial standards.

This book has been carefully designed to minimise awkward
page turns and to make playing from it a real pleasure.

Particular care has been given to specifying acid-free, neutral-sized paper
made from pulps which have not been elemental chlorine bleached.
This pulp is from farmed sustainable forests and
was produced with special regard for the environment.

Throughout, the printing and binding have been planned to ensure a sturdy,
attractive publication which should give years of enjoyment.

If your copy fails to meet our high standards,
please inform us and we will gladly replace it.

www.musicsales.com

Playing With Scales:
The Concept

Playing With Scales is a new educational resource designed to help young musicians play their scales. It consists of a series of fun accompaniments for scales and arpeggios, written to cover the keys and scale patterns required by the instrument. Teachers can accompany their students in lessons and then students can practise their scales at home with audio downloaded using the unique card enclosed in the back of the book.

Playing With Scales can help the student in several ways. Playing over an accompaniment will help with timing, as part of the challenge with playing scales is to get them to flow evenly from one note to the next. Intonation will also benefit. Most importantly of all, the actual experience of playing scales will be enriched. Scales will no longer feel dry and disembodied, as they now become part of a piece of music. The accompaniments have been written in a wide variety of styles, to suit all tastes and moods. Various tonalities are also explored. Some accompaniments are not even in the same key as the scale; a major scale can sit quite nicely over an accompaniment that is in the relative minor, for example. The aim of *Playing With Scales* is to engage the imagination of the student, and ultimately, *to make scale practice fun!*

Playing With Scales:
Clarinet, Level One

This volume contains accompaniments for scales and arpeggios required at the first level of playing. Each scale has a series of accompaniments, which present the student with a range of different styles and moods. All the accompaniments are available as audio downloads, but can also be played by a teacher in lessons. *Playing With Scales* therefore becomes an interactive tool for use in a student's lesson.

C major scale

F major scale

♩ = 50   Track 5

♩ = 50   Track 6

♩ = 60   Track 7

♩ = 66   Track 8

F major arpeggio

Track 12

Track 13

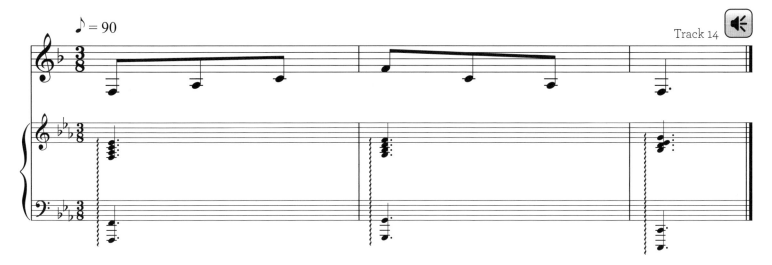

Track 14

G major scale

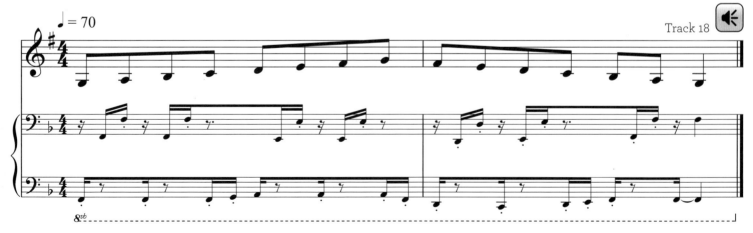

G major arpeggio

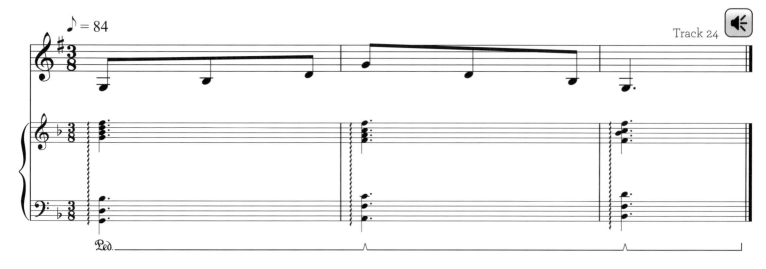

A minor harmonic scale

A minor melodic scale

A minor natural scale

A minor arpeggio

123456789

HOW TO DOWNLOAD YOUR MUSIC TRACKS

1. Carefully remove your Download Card from the inside back cover of this book.

2. On the back of the card is your unique access code. Enter this at www.musicsalesdownloads.com

TO REDEEM THIS CARD VISIT
www.musicsalesdownloads.com

ENTER ACCESS CODE:

XXXXXXXXXX

Download Cards are powered by Dropcards.
User must accept terms at dropcards.com/terms
which are adopted by The Music Sales Group.
Not redeemable for cash. Void where prohibited or restricted by law.

DCARD1006478

Opening mad world.mp3 ☒

You have chosen to open:

♫ Mad World.mp3

    which is a: MPEG Layer 3 Audio (3.58MB)
    from: http://s3.amazonaws.com

What should Firefox do with this file?

○ Open with   iTunes (default)   ▾

◉ Save File

☐ Do this automatically for files like this from now on.

     OK   Cancel

3. Follow the instructions to save your files to your computer*. That's it!

*Appearance of download manager will vary depending upon operating system and web browser.
In case of difficulty when downloading files, please contact dropcards.com/help
Card missing? Please contact music@musicsales.co.uk